Copyright ©2020 Bonnie Belden-Doney

All Scripture quotations are from The Passion Translation®. Copyright © 2017, 2018 by Passion & Fire Ministries, Inc. Used by permission. All rights reserved. ThePassionTranslation.com.

Scripture quotations taken from the Amplified® Bible (AMPC),Copyright © 1954, 1958, 1962, 1964, 1965, 1987 by The Lockman Foundation Used by permission. www.Lockman.org

Artwork Cover by Bonnie Belden-Doney

www.bonniebelden-doney.com

Graphic design and layout by

Bonnie Belden-Doney and Lisa Stone Pettis

ISBN: 9798674214342

Printed in the USA

dedication

To my husband, Dave who lovingly and patiently answered unending questions. His undying love for me and joy he brings sets me free to pursue my dream.

To my sister Jan who always stands beside me.

To my son Paul, in his gracious ways, continues to support and give me hope to go forward.

To my dear daughter-in-law, Lisa. I want to say thank you from the bottom of my heart for her insight and knowledge of the publishing world. Her knowledge and support is reflected on the pages of this journal.

BONNIE BELDEN-DONEY

Safe & Secure

Safe & Secure

Jesus replied,
"And my Father will love you
so deeply that we will come to you
and make you our dwelling place."
John 14:23b tpt

BONNIE BELDEN-DONEY

a note from bonnie

Safe & Secure is a daily journal that will enhance your journey with the Lord in discovering how to stay in the secret dwelling place with Him. Through all of life's happenings there is comfort in knowing that we can go to the dwelling place each day and know that the Lord is waiting with anticipation. He wants us to discover His great loving care for us. It is in His dwelling place where He invites us to come in and sit for awhile.

table of contents

Psalm 91 - Jesus our Strength

Psalm 23 - Jesus our Shepherd

Psalm 23 - Jesus our Defender

"When you sit enthroned under the shadow of Shaddai… you are hidden in the strength of God Most High."

Psalm 91:1

Sitting under the the shadow of The Almighty God you are hidden in His strength. It is the most safe and secure place to begin your walk every day.

What circumstances are you facing today that make you want to run and hide?

Can you sit in under His Shadow?

What strength do you need in the safety of God Most High?

Reflections

Prayer Requests

Thank you, Lord

"He's the hope that holds me and the Stronghold to shelter me, the only God for me, and my great confidence."

Psalm 91:2

Hope is tangible.
Does your heart hope for things that you cannot see? Often times we grasp for hope, tring to make things happen.

Do you allow yourself to trust in the hope of the Lord?   He is your hope and He is your Stronghold to shelter you.

Will you allow Him to become your only God for hope and a shelter?

Reflections

"He will rescue you from every hidden trap of the enemy".

Psalm 91:3 _{TPT}

Have you been in a situation where you needed to be rescued but you didn't know who could help you? Bombardment from the enemy is overwhelming, creating a feeling of hopelessness. No matter where the enemy's trap has been set and hidden, the Lord will rescue you.

When have you been in a place where you needed the Lord to rescue you?

Reflections

Prayer Requests

Thank you, Lord

> "...he will protect you from false accusation and any deadly curse."

Psalm 91:3.b _TPT_

Words spoken bring life or death. Often times the words spoken are in haste without giving thought to any of the consequences. Are there places and times when you have spoken words in haste that have caused others pain? Are there times when words have broken your heart and it has had a ripple effect of unforgiveness?

Have you allowed the Word of the Lord to protect you from the accusations and deadly curses?

Reflections

Prayer Requests

Thank you, Lord

"His massive arms are wrapped around you, protecting you".

Psalm 91:4 a _{TPT}

Safety and security are in the loving, protective arms of the Lord. So many times we run from these protective arms when we feel we can handle it all on our own. Have you tried to protect yourself from harm and danger discovering that you are incapable of doing it alone?

Have you discovered that He really wants to protect you and you don't have to be alone in your journey?

Reflections

Prayer Requests

Thank you, Lord

"You can run under his covering
of majesty and hide."

Psalm 91:4.b TPT

Many times we have needed mercy and grace extended to us even though we feel unworthy, not ever wanting to stand before our King with mud on our faces and our clothes all tattered from the struggle. Yet, our King Jesus, takes his robe of righteousness and wraps it tightly around our shoulders, hiding our shame.
Have you ever been in a place in your life where you just needed mercy extended?
Do you need a place to hide?

Reflections

Prayer Requests

Thank you, Lord

"His arms of faithfulness
are a shield
keeping you from harm."

Psalm 91:4.c

Faithful warrior, friend.
He is faithful in all He does and
faithful in who He is for you.
If you consider the word faithful
you might think that being faithful
requires much more than you can
comprehend due to the fact that
you don't think you are faithful.
He is your shield and guide.

Will you allow Him to
be your shield?

Reflections

Prayer Requests

Thank you, Lord

"You will never worry about an attack of demonic forces at night nor have to fear a spirit of darkness coming against you."

Psalm 91:5 TPT

There is no fear in the secret place of the Lord, under the shelter of His arms.

Do you run to the secret place with the Lord when fear tries to overwhelm you?

Have you taken on the fear and let it control your situation?

Reflections

Prayer Requests

Thank you, Lord

"Don't fear a thing!
Whether by night or by day,
demonic danger will not trouble you,
nor will the powers of evil be
launched against you."
Psalm 91:6 TPT

Fear separates us from the true
Love of our King.

Have you chosen the lie of fear?

Do you want to live in the lie
of fear instead of knowing that
when we stand in the Love of the
King we can be free from fear?

Reflections

Prayer Requests

Thank you, Lord

"Even in a time of disaster, with thousands and thousands being killed, you will remain unscathed and unharmed."

Psalm 91:7 TPT

Protection comes from the Lord in the secret place under the shadow of His wings.

When you see a disaster happening around you are you assured that you are protected in the secret place with the Lord?

Do you trust in the safety of His protection?

Reflections

Prayer Requests

Thank you, Lord

> "You will be a spectator as the wicked
> perish in judgment,
> for they will be paid back
> for what they have done!"
> Psalm 91:8

The advantage of being in the
secret place is the ability to be
a spectator of the demise of the
enemy as it takes place.
The quiet place with the Lord
allows you to sit in
His presence and watch his protection.

Have you ever longed to watch the
enemy be defeated in areas of your life?

What area in your life needs to be
defeated and perish in judgement?

Reflections

Prayer Requests

Thank you, Lord

"When we live our lives within the shadow of God Most High, our secret hiding place, we will always be shielded from harm..."

Psalm 91:9  TPT

The Shadow of our Lord
is our secret hiding place.
Staying under the shadow of
our protector can present
challenges to our way of
thinking and doing things.

Have you ever thought that you
could make it through the day
by stepping out on your own
because you knew it would be ok?

What did you learn when you
tried to do it by yourself?

Reflections

Prayer Requests

Thank you, Lord

> "When we live our lives within the shadow of God Most High,...
> How then could evil prevail against us or disease infect us?"
>
> Psalm 91:9 & 10

In His Presence there is protection. Living within the shadow of God allows God to be all He wants to be for us.
Our Protector, our Provider, our Shield, our Defense and the more we stay under the shadow the deeper and more intimate we become with Him. He wants to be all to us.

There are times when we think we don't need to be under the shadow, how has that worked out for you?

Reflections

Prayer Requests

Thank you, Lord

"God sends angels with special
orders to protect you wherever you
go, defending you from all harm."

Psalm 91:11 *TPT*

God is faithful
to instill hope and confidence
in His care into your life.
He has created his angels to protect
you and defend you from harm.

Have you been in a position
where you know that the angels
of the Lord have been dispatched
to protect and defend you?

Reflections

"If you walk into a trap, they
(the angels) will be there for you
and keep you from stumbling."

Psalm 91:12 TPT

God's angels are watching over
you even when you step into a
trap. They keep you from falling.

Have you been in a situation where
you felt trapped with no way out?

At that time, did you know the angels
kept you from stumbling headlong?

Reflections

Prayer Requests

Thank you, Lord

"You'll even walk unharmed among the fiercest powers of darkness, trampling every one of them beneath your feet!"

Psalm 91:13 *TPT*

His presence is all encompassing bringing peace and safety. At the darkest times, facing the fierest of enemies, the Lord has given you the strength and tenacity to trample them under your feet. Unharmed.

Do you take into consideration all of the times when you have been unharmed in a frightful situation?

Reflections

Prayer Requests

Thank you, Lord

"For here is what the Lord has spoken to me: Because you have delighted in me as my great lover, I will greatly protect you."

Psalm 91:14 *TPT*

The Lord is so pleased with your love for Him He protects you. He loves to be loved. He protects His love for you.

What would compel you to delight in the Lord?

Would it be all of the things that He offers you or is it because you love Him so dearly?

Reflections

Prayer Requests

Thank you, Lord

"I will greatly protect you.
I will set you in a high place,
safe and secure before my face."

Psalm 91:14b TPT

The Lord picks you up and puts you
in a safe and secure place
before Him.

Are there times when have
needed someone to protect you
and place you in secure places?

Or do you say to yourself, "I
can do this on my own"?
Ask yourself if you are willing to
allow the Lord to protect you.

Reflections

Prayer Requests

Thank you, Lord

"I will answer your cry for help
every time you pray, and you
will find and feel my presence."

Psalm 91:15 TPT

Not only does the Lord hear
your cry when you pray, you will
know He is present with you.
Finding the Lord is a
matter of communion with
Him on a consistant basis.
He is ever present.

Will you invite Him to be your
constant companion?

Reflections

Prayer Requests

Thank you, Lord

"...even in your time
of pressure and trouble.
I will be your glorious hero
and give you a feast."

Psalm 91:15b TPT

Just sit at the table of His presense
and allow Him to be your Hero.
Pressure and trouble draw us deeper
into the secret place of the Lord.

What keeps you closer to the Lord?

Is it what He can give to you or
who He is as your glorious hero?

Reflections

Prayer Requests

Thank you, Lord

"You will be satisfied
with a full life and
with all that I do for you."

Psalm 91:16 TPT

Satisfaction in life comes in all that the Lord does for you. Many times one may think that satifaction comes with owning things, accomplishing goals and many times they are done with our own efforts. The Lord has given us an option to be satified with all that He wants to do for us.

Is there a time when have you have said to yourself, "if I just finish this one thing, I think I will be satified", but the dissatifation sneaks back in to haunt you?

Reflections

Prayer Requests

_____
_____
_____
_____
_____
_____
_____
_____

Thank you, Lord

_____
_____
_____
_____
_____
_____
_____

*"For you will enjoy the
fullness of my salvation!"*

Psalm 91:16 b _{TPT}

In the secret dwelling place,
next to the heart of God,
He has given us His joy
in the fullness of
His salvation.
Therefore, taking our place
to receive this enjoyment is a choice.

What keeps you in the secret place so
you can enjoy the Lord's salvation?

Reflections

Prayer Requests

Thank you, Lord

"The Lord is my best
friend and my Shepherd."

Psalm 23:1 TPT

The Lord is a faithful friend
who always watches over us.
He keeps us from harm as does a
shepherd who looks after his sheep.

Are there times in your life when
you have not been a faithful friend?

In those times were you able
to resolve the friendship?

Have you allowed the Lord
to be a friend?

Reflections

Prayer Requests

Thank you, Lord

"I always have more than enough."

Psalm 23:1 b _{TPT}

The Lord makes sure that there is more
than enough provision for each day.
His provision is not only in the
tangible things we see or possess,
but also for the soul and spirit.
Often times we have a mindset of
provision with the things we
can see, touch or possess.

Are there times when you
become anxious in what appears
to be lack in areas in your life?

Reflections

Prayer Requests

Thank you, Lord

"He offers a resting place
for me in his luxurious love."

Psalm 23:2 TPT

We have the opportunity to receive
rest and peace in His love and heart.
This love is all encompassing.

Describe times when you have known
the all encompassing love of the Lord
in a place where you needed it most.

What questions would you
ask your best friend, Jesus?

Reflections

Prayer Requests

Thank you, Lord

*"His tracks take me
to an oasis of peace,
the quiet brook of bliss."*

Psalm 23:2 b ₜₚₜ

Following the steps of The Shepherd will take us to peaceful, quiet places. Waters of rest and restoration that soothe the weary in heart and soul. So many times we want to lead our lives and not follow.

What is the Holy Spirit saying to you about following Him to the oasis of peace and the quiet brook?

Reflections

Prayer Requests

Thank you, Lord

*"That's where he restores
and revives my life."*

Psalm 23:3 _{TPT}

Lost and broken in the way of life?
Restoration in the lost and
broken ways of life begin
beside the quiet brooks.
The Lord invites us to
follow Him to the still waters.
There He brings the restoration
of life and revies our heart. Lost
and broken areas in our lives often
hold us in the drama of despair.

Think about following the Lord
to the still waters. What would
keep you from the still waters?

Reflections

Prayer Requests

Thank you, Lord

"He opens before me pathways to God's pleasure and leads me along in his footsteps of righteousness so that I can bring honor to his name."

Psalm 23:3 b

The path of the Lord
is open for His pleasure.
His love leads us by
showing us His footsteps.
He walks in righteousness
because He is righteous.
It is because of His righteousness we
walk and bring honor to His name.
Where is the Holy Spirit calling you to walk?

Have you seen a path laid
out in front of you?
Hint: Take a look at His footsteps.
Choose His footsteps.

Reflections

Prayer Requests

Thank you, Lord

"Lord, even when your path takes me
through the valley of deepest darkness,
fear will never conquer me,
for you already have!"

Psalm 23:4 TPT

Steep canyon walls on either
side, that are closing in on you.
The darkness is closing in and you
feel the terror of the darkness.
The faithful covering of love and
peace of the Lord has conquered
all fear. Fear cannot conquer you.

Is the valley so deep that you
cannot feel anything but fear?
Can you feel His presence
in the valley?
Can you feel Him hold you?

Reflections

Prayer Requests

Thank you, Lord

"You remain close to me and
lead me through it all the way. "

Psalm 23:4 b

Jesus said He will never
leave you or forsake you.
There is never a time when He has
left you to struggle in life by yourself.
He walks through it all with
you. Abandonment can make you
feel thrown out to the wolves.
This causes you to feel unsafe and
insecure, struggling with everything.

Where do you go when
you feel abandoned?
Do you struggle with
allowing the Lord to lead you?

Reflections

Prayer Requests

Thank you, Lord

> "Your authority is my strength
> and my peace. The comfort of
> your love takes away my fear.
> I'll never be lonely, for you are near."
>
> Psalm 23:4c *TPT*

Because of Who He is,
as our Shepherd King,
we will take comfort in Him,
assured in the truth that He is our
strength and our peace. Thus we
can know that He can take away
our fear and we are never alone.
When His strength is present there is
comfort in knowing we have a strong
place to stand and it gives us peace.

Was there a time in your life
that you have felt the strong
presence of the Lord in which you
could trust and not be afraid?

Reflections

Prayer Requests

Thank you, Lord

"You become my delicious feast
even when my
enemies dare to fight."

Psalm 23:5 TPT

At His table we are fed with the joy
of His Presence. Our lives become full.
We enjoy Him in the presence of our
enemies. They cannot touch us
because they are held, at bay,
outside the Presence of the Lord.
Safety and security come to us when
we partake in the feast of the Lord.

What are you feasting on when
you come into His presence?

The enemies will try to join you,
but they are not invited.

Reflections

Prayer Requests

Thank you, Lord

"You anoint me with the
fragrance of your Holy Spirit;
you give me all I can drink of you
until my heart overflows."

Psalm 23:5 b_{TPT}

The Holy Spirit fills us with His
fragrant peace until our heart
is healed. He fills us to overflowing
so that others will be touched
by His Presence.
There is an undeniable presence when
we allow the Holy Spirit to anoint us.
We are full yet feel like we are
empty and hunger for more.
Seeking and partnering with
the Holy Spirit brings us into
the secret place of intimacy.
What is the cry of your heart?

Reflections

Prayer Requests

Thank you, Lord

"So why would I fear the future?"

Psalm 23:6 *TPT*

There is no fear in the
Love of the Lord.
So, if there is no fear in the
love of the Lord then we
should never fear the future.
We have been promised
today. Looking to the
future is the Lord's business.
Living in today takes the
anxeity out of tomorrow.

Ask the Lord who
He wants to be for you today.

Reflections

Prayer Requests

Thank you, Lord

> "For your goodness and love
> pursue me all the days of my life.
> Then afterward, when my life is
> through, I'll return to your glorious
> presence to be forever with you!"
>
> Psalm 23:6 b *TPT*

The Lord's goodness and love will
never stop chasing us down
to bring to us His love.
His pursuit is endless.
Every day of our lives He brings
to us love and goodness.
It is in our willinness to
receive this wonderful gift but
there are times in our lives
when our receiver is broken.

He is there. Can you receive?

Reflections

Prayer Requests

Thank you, Lord

"The Lord is my revelation-light
to guide me along the way; he's the
source of my salvation to defend
me every day.   I fear no one!"

Psalm 27:1 *TPT*

The Lord is a constant light,
never leaving us in the
darkness of despair and fear.
His arm of salvation is always
there to defend us and protect.

Why should we be afraid of
the enemy of our souls?
The Lord's wrap around presence
engulfs us every day.

When you begin to feel the
despair and fear overtake you,
can you remind yourself that the
Lord's arms are ever present?

Reflections

Prayer Requests

Thank you, Lord

"I'll never turn back and
run from you, Lord;
surround and protect me."

Psalm 27:1 b TPT

Our Defender! Our Strong Tower!
How could we ever turn
and run from Him? We will allow
Him to surround and protect us.
Even in the valley of the shadow (it is
only a shadow soon to be dispelled by
the light of the His Presence) of death
we will remember that the Lord is a
constant protector and defender.
He is the strength of our life.

Has your strength been drained in a trial?
Have you pressed into the
arms of the Defender?

Reflections

Prayer Requests

Thank you, Lord

"When evil ones come
to destroy me,
they will be the ones who turn back."

Psalm 27:2 *TPT*

It is because of the Presence of the Lord,
that our enemy will turn
back from their pursuit.
The enemy of our souls cannot stay
where the Presence of the Lord resides.
They stumble and fall.

We stand and watch as we
allow the Lord to be our
Defender. He is asking us to stay in
His Presence close to His heart.
He longs to surround us.

Have you allowed Him to be the
Defender by staying close to His heart?

Reflections

Prayer Requests

Thank you, Lord

> "My heart will not be afraid
> even if an army rises to attack.
> I know that you are there for
> me, so I will not be shaken."
>
> Psalm 27:3  TPT

Fear is a distressing emotion aroused by impending danger, evil, pain, whether the threat is real or imagined. The feeling of being afraid causes feelings of dread or apprehension. Fear can often make us feel paralysed when the enemy rises to attack. The Lord is reassuring us that in the midst of the feeling of fear, we will not be shaken because the Lord is with us and He is there for us.

Are you confident in the fact that the Lord is always there?

Reflections

Prayer Requests

Thank you, Lord

"Here's the one thing I crave from God, the one thing I seek above all else: I want the privilege of living with him every moment in his house."

Psalm 27:4 TPT

To crave; to hunger, have a strong desire, to demand.
Often times we dismiss the feeling of craving because we may think it is selfish. But King David's heart was so hungry for the Presence of the Lord that he was persistant in his pursuit of dwelling in the Presence of the Lord every day of his life.

What stirs up the craving and hunger to be in the Presence of the Lord?

Reflections

Prayer Requests

Thank you, Lord

"I want the privilege of living with him every moment in his house, finding the sweet loveliness of his face, filled with awe, delighting in his glory and grace."

Psalm 27:4 b^{TPT}

It is a privilege to live in the Presence of the Lord and to dwell consistently in His house.
The secret dwelling place with the Lord opens our eyes and heart to see the beauty of the Lord.
The sweet attractiveness and delightful loveliness of the Lord is what we crave.
The constant pursuit, on our part, is to stay every moment in the secret place.

Do we find ourselves in a position of requiring answers to our prayers more that requiring our hearts to crave and long for the Beauty of His Presence?

Reflections

Prayer Requests

Thank you, Lord

"I want to live my life so close to him
that he takes pleasure in
my every prayer."

Psalm 27:4 TPT

The Lord is so pleased when we stay in the secret dwelling place with Him. He loves our conversations with Him. Our friend, our closest confidant, the keeper of our tears. This precious relationship with the Lord creates a security in us that we know the deep heart beat of His heart. We can ask Him anything because He loves the consistent fellowship. Relationship. Has the Lord been calling you into the secret place of relationship? A place of hearing His heart because you sit next to Him in safety?

Reflections

Prayer Requests

Thank you, Lord

"In His shelter in the day of trouble, that's where you'll find me, for He hides me there in His holiness."

Psalm 27:5 TPT

Shelter in place. So many times we hear this phrase when a storm is coming or an enemy is out to destroy. Sheltering in place in the day of trouble should be our daily stance in life. Sheltering in the secret dwelling place is where we will find the Lord. He hides us in His Holiness. It is His Holiness that we are guarded from the enemy and his bombardment of lies that bring in fear. Often we run to our own outside sources to find shelter. Where do you see yourself running to, to be safe and secure?

Reflections

Prayer Requests

Thank you, Lord

> "He has smuggled me into his secret place, where I'm kept safe and secure—out of reach from all my enemies."
>
> Psalm 27:5 b

Have you ever hidden a precious heirloom in a secret place so no one could find it except you? The Lord hides us in His secret place to keep us safe and secure from the enemy of our soul. He snatches us out of the reach of the enemy and keeps us hidden. Because of His love for us, He calls us daily to stay in the secret place of safety. But when we become bombarded by the tatics of the enemy, He pulls us into the safe and secure place. Look at the times when the Lord has hidden you.

Reflections

Prayer Requests

Thank you, Lord

> "Triumphant now, I'll bring him
> my offerings of praise, singing and
> shouting with ecstatic joy!
> Yes, listen and you can hear the
> fanfare my shouts of praise to the Lord!"
>
> Psalm 27:6

We can lift up our head and turn our eyes to the One who has redeemed our life from destruction. When we think about the Lord and his goodness and kindness to us our hearts are filled with praise, singing and shouting. We are triumphant in life because of the Lord. Destruction of our lives is not in God's plan for us.

There are days when our lives are filled with sorrow and fear, but in those times do we find ourselves rejoicing in Who He is and what He has done for us?

Reflections

Prayer Requests

Thank you, Lord

> "God, hear my cry.
> Show me your grace.
> Show me mercy, and
> send the help I need!"
> Psalm 27:7 TPT

Listening is a skill that most of us must learn. It requires diligence on our part to hear what another person is trying to say. But, the Lord always listens when we cry for help. He hears your cry and has extended His grace and mercy. His mercies are new every morning so there are no left overs from the day before. He is ever present in our time of need.

Can you rest in the fact that God hears your cry?

Reflections

Prayer Requests

Thank you, Lord

"Lord, when you said to me,
"Seek my face," my inner
being responded, "I'm seeking
your face with all my heart."

Psalm 27:8 TPT

The Lord is making a request of us to come
requiring His presence
to see His face and
requiring His presence as our vital need.
The Holy Spirit woos us with His
kindness and His heart is open
to receive our relationship.

Does your spirit respond to His call to
come into the secret place to see His face?

Reflections

Prayer Requests

Thank you, Lord

> "So don't hide yourself, Lord, when I come to find you. You're the God of my salvation; how can you reject your servant in anger?"
>
> Psalm 27:9

What would cause the Lord to hide His face when we come to Him? He has always been available we say. He has never forsaken us, yet the feeling that He will hide His face when we come to Him. Our feeling of unworthiness, hidden sin and iniquity will lie to us and tell us the Lord will hide His face. Yet, He has stated we can run to Him and hide in Him, asking forgiveness. He will never abandon us. We abandon Him because of guilt. We overcome by boldly coming into His presence in the saftey of the secret place.

Reflections

Prayer Requests

Thank you, Lord

"You've been my only hope, so don't forsake me now when I need you!"

Psalm 27:9 b *TPT*

Hope. Expectation in knowing that the Lord will not forsake us. With trepdition and fear knocking at the door, we turn our hearts to the only One who offers us hope. We know that in our time of need He will not forsake us. His promises are true and unending. Many times we base our feelings on what we see or hear, but the Lord says, "don't be moved by what you see or hear but be moved by what I say." Trust in the Lord.

What causes us to hope in the Lord knowing he will not forsake us?

Reflections

Prayer Requests

Thank you, Lord

> "My father and mother
> abandoned me. I'm like an orphan!
> But you took me in
> and made me yours."
>
> Psalm 27:10 TPT

Abandonment:
deserted, neglected, and stranded. Fathers and mothers, as well meaning as they may be, will abandon us in one or more areas of our lives. They don't have the capability to meet all of our needs. But the Lord adopts us and makes us His own because he can be all to us that our parents were lacking. We learn to allow the Lord to take us into His presence and create a safe place for our hearts and souls. Often times abandonment will try to overcome us. How do we overcome?

Reflections

Prayer Requests

Thank you, Lord

"Now teach me all about your ways and tell me what to do. Make it clear for me to understand, for I am surrounded by waiting enemies."

Psalm 27:11 *TPT*

The ways of the Lord are learned in the secret place. He is the Teacher Lord. When we quiet ourselves before Him we learn what He is telling us and where to walk and how to live our lives. His ways are clear for us to understand. Our enemies are always waiting on the sidelines to try and distract us away from His ways. They will try to entice us to look away from the path of the Lord. Our ways are not the Lord's ways because His are greater.

What entices you to stray away from the path of the Lord?

Reflections

Prayer Requests

Thank you, Lord

> "Don't let them defeat me, Lord.
> You can't let me fall into their clutches!
> They keep accusing me of
> things I've never done while
> they plot evil against me."
>
> Psalm 27:12 TPT

The Lord Defender is standing by our side when the enemy comes to accuse and engulf us with his accusations and evil plots. But the Lord will not let them defeat us because He is our Defender. No weapon that the enemy can form against us will prosper. Every word that he speaks against us we can turn those words back to him. The Lord has given us the power to stand against the enemy in full force. He stands with us and the enemy cannot stay. Are you willing to allow the Lord to be your Defender?

Reflections

Prayer Requests

Thank you, Lord

"Yet I totally trust you to rescue me
one more time, so that I can
see once again how good you
are while I'm still alive!"

Psalm 27:13 *TPT*

We may ask the question, in
times of the storms, "Where
would I be if I had not seen
the Lord's goodness
extended to me while I live?"
He is always good and
His kindness chases me down.
He stands with me. Protects me.
Guides me. Gives me breath each
day. He is faithful and kind.
Praising the Lord through the trials,
knowing that fear has no
place in our lives.

Worship Him for all He
has done for you.

Reflections

Prayer Requests

Thank you, Lord

> "Here's what I've learned
> through it all:
> Don't give up; don't be impatient;
> be entwined as one with the Lord."
>
> Psalm 27:14 _{TPT}

Be diligent in and through the trials, knowing that the Lord our Shepherd, our Defender, our Strong Tower give us the tenancity to continue in the secret place with Him. He calls us to a strong, close relationship with Him, where we will be persistent in only saying what He says and doing what He tells us to do.

Choices come to us on a daily basis to live in the secret place, under the Shadow of His wing, are you willing to take the challenge?

Reflections

Prayer Requests

Thank you, Lord

"Be brave and courageous,
and never lose hope.
Yes, keep on waiting for he
will never disappoint you!"

Psalm 27:14 b

Our Encouager, Jesus calls us to be brave and courageous. We place our hope in Him, with patience knowing that He has a plan for our lives on a daily basis. He never leaves us or forsakes us. We can trust Him for every area of our lives. There is no fear in the love of the Lord. He has called us to live in the Secret Dwelling Place with Him which offers us saftey and security.

Meet the Lord today in the most safe place of all, next to His heart.

Reflections

Prayer Requests

Thank you, Lord

Prayer Requests

Thank you, Lord

Made in the USA
Middletown, DE
24 September 2020